# CULTIVATING SUCCESS IN UNCERTAINTY

A Comprehensive Handbook
for Entrepreneurs

Traci Fischer

Copyright © 2023 Traci Fischer

# CONTENTS

# Introduction

In a world characterized by rapid change and unforeseeable challenges, entrepreneurs stand as modern-day pioneers, boldly venturing into uncharted territory. They are the visionaries, the risk-takers, and the architects of the future, relentlessly pursuing opportunities amid the ever-shifting sands of uncertainty.

This book, "Cultivating Success in Uncertainty: A Comprehensive Handbook for Entrepreneurs," is your guiding light in this labyrinthine entrepreneurial landscape. Here, we embark on a transformative journey, seeking not only to survive but to flourish amidst the unknown. As we dive into the pages that follow, we'll unravel the secrets to resilience, adaptability, and innovation—essential traits that will shape your entrepreneurial path.

In an age where the only constant is change, it's the entrepreneurial mindset that sets you apart. You'll discover that this mindset is more than just a buzzword; it's a vital compass, guiding you through the turbulent waters of innovation and enterprise. We'll delve into the deep recesses of this mindset, uncovering the resilience to face adversity, the creativity to solve complex problems, and the courage to challenge the status quo.

The journey begins with your visionary exploration, where you'll learn to craft and refine your entrepreneurial vision, setting your sights on a destination unknown to most. We'll equip you with the tools to discern opportunities where others see chaos and to set audacious goals that spark your entrepreneurial fire.

Uncertainty is your constant companion on this voyage. But don't worry; we're prepared. We'll navigate the treacherous waters of risk and unpredictability, charting a course that balances daring leaps with calculated steps. You'll become a master of decision-making in the face of ambiguity, ensuring that every move you make is purposeful.

In entrepreneurship, the journey is not solitary. You'll assemble a dream team that complements your skills and shares your ambition. Together, you'll foster a culture of innovation and adaptability, laying the foundation for success. As we traverse these challenging landscapes, you'll learn to create value in the very midst of chaos, developing groundbreaking products and services that meet the dynamic needs of a rapidly evolving world.

Financing your venture can be a daunting task, especially when the ground beneath your feet is constantly shifting. We'll explore the myriad ways to secure funding for your startup and equip you with the financial savvy required to manage your resources effectively. You'll emerge with the confidence to weather the storms of cash flow and emerge stronger on the other side.

Marketing your brand in uncertain times requires a strategic approach. We'll guide you through the process of building a brand and crafting a marketing strategy in dynamic markets. You'll harness the power of digital marketing, social media, and emerging trends to engage your audience. Building and sustaining enduring customer relationships will be your hallmark.

As your entrepreneurial expedition progresses, we'll help you scale your success while preserving the core values that define your venture. Growth, scalability, and ongoing innovation will be your watchwords, and you'll be prepared to meet the new challenges that every milestone presents.

But perhaps the most vital lesson of all is to embrace failure and view it as a stepping stone to success. The setbacks you encounter will be transformed into invaluable lessons, nourishing a culture of continuous improvement within your organization. Here, you'll understand that resilience is not just a desirable trait but a vital one.

The final leg of our journey takes us through the ever-changing landscape of uncertain times, where we'll navigate economic, social, and technological shifts with poise and determination. You'll emerge with the knowledge and strategies needed to secure long-term sustainability and impact not only in your industry but in the broader world.

This is your invitation to a transformative journey—a handbook designed to empower and embolden entrepreneurs in the face of the unknown. The world may be uncertain, but in these pages, you'll find the certainty of a well-charted course to entrepreneurial success. As we set sail into the uncharted waters of entrepreneurship, remember that the possibilities are as boundless as your vision, and the adventure begins now.

# Chapter 1: The Entrepreneurial Mindset

In the realm of entrepreneurship, where uncertainty is a constant companion and change is the only certainty, success often hinges on more than just a brilliant idea or a well-executed plan. It's the entrepreneurial mindset that truly separates the triumphant from the struggling, the pioneers from the cautious, and the game-changers from the sideline watchers. This chapter delves into the very essence of the entrepreneurial mindset, exploring its key components and revealing why it's the bedrock of thriving in uncertainty.

## The Essence of the Entrepreneurial Mindset

At its core, the entrepreneurial mindset is a distinct way of thinking, a set of attitudes, beliefs, and cognitive patterns that shape an entrepreneur's approach to challenges, opportunities, and the unknown. This mindset is not a static trait but an evolving quality, one that can be cultivated and refined over time. It is characterized by several fundamental attributes:

### 1. Adaptability

Entrepreneurs thrive on change and adapt to it with ease. They embrace the idea that the business landscape is in perpetual flux, and instead of resisting change, they welcome it. This adaptability is a crucial trait that allows them to pivot when necessary, experiment with new ideas, and adjust strategies swiftly in response to shifting circumstances.

## 2. Resilience

Resilience is the capacity to bounce back from adversity, and entrepreneurs encounter their fair share of setbacks. However, they view these setbacks not as failures but as valuable lessons that propel them forward. A resilient mindset helps entrepreneurs persevere in the face of challenges, maintaining their determination and enthusiasm.

## 3. Creativity

Entrepreneurs are inherently creative. They see solutions where others see problems and constantly search for innovative ways to meet market needs. Their creative thinking leads to disruptive ideas and groundbreaking products or services.

## 4. Risk-Taking

Risk is an inherent part of entrepreneurship, and a healthy appetite for calculated risk-taking is a hallmark of the entrepreneurial mindset. Entrepreneurs understand that calculated risks can yield significant rewards, and they're willing to step out of their comfort zones to seize opportunities.

## 5. Optimism

A positive outlook is a driving force behind the entrepreneurial mindset. Entrepreneurs maintain a hopeful attitude even in the face of adversity, believing in their ability to overcome challenges and create a brighter future.

This optimism fuels their persistence and resilience.

## 6. Vision

Entrepreneurs are guided by a clear and compelling vision. This vision serves as a beacon, illuminating the path forward, motivating the team, and ensuring that every decision and action aligns with their long-term goals.

### Nurturing the Entrepreneurial Mindset

The entrepreneurial mindset is not solely the domain of the born entrepreneur. It can be nurtured and developed by anyone willing to embark on the journey. Here are some strategies to cultivate and strengthen this mindset:

### 1. Embrace Continuous Learning

Entrepreneurs are perpetual learners. They seek out new knowledge, both inside and outside their field, and remain open to new ideas and perspectives. Reading, attending workshops, and networking are all part of their commitment to ongoing education.

### 2. Surround Yourself with Inspiration

Your environment plays a crucial role in shaping your mindset. Surround yourself with people who inspire and challenge you, whether they are fellow entrepreneurs, mentors, or thought leaders. Their perspectives and experiences can be invaluable in nurturing your mindset.

### 3. Cultivate Resilience

Resilience can be cultivated through practice. When faced with challenges, view them as opportunities for growth. Develop a habit of analyzing setbacks, extracting lessons from them, and moving forward with renewed determination.

### 4. Encourage Risk-Taking

In your personal and professional life, seek out opportunities to take calculated risks. Start small and gradually expand your comfort zone. By stepping into the unknown, you'll develop your risk-taking muscles.

### 5. Stay Curious

Curiosity is a driving force behind creativity. Ask questions, explore new ideas, and challenge assumptions. Cultivate the habit of seeking out different perspectives and thinking outside the box.

### 6. Define Your Vision

Your vision is your North Star. Take the time to define a compelling, long-term vision for your entrepreneurial journey. This vision will guide your decisions and actions, keeping you focused on the big picture.

### The Entrepreneurial Mindset in Practice

To illustrate the power of the entrepreneurial mindset in

practice, let's consider the story of Sarah, a budding entrepreneur in the tech industry. Sarah had a vision of creating an innovative mobile app to help people lead healthier lives. She possessed a strong entrepreneurial mindset, which manifested in her journey:

- Adaptability: When her initial app concept faced challenges, Sarah pivoted and transformed it into a health and fitness platform, capitalizing on the burgeoning wellness market.

- Resilience:She encountered technical glitches, funding roadblocks, and competition. However, each obstacle strengthened her resolve, and she persevered through each setback.

- Creativity: Sarah constantly brainstormed and sought unique features that would set her app apart. This creativity led to a groundbreaking feature that catapulted her platform's success.

- Risk-Taking:Sarah took the risk of leaving her stable job to pursue her entrepreneurial dream. Her willingness to embrace this uncertainty paid off as her startup gained traction.

- Optimism: Despite setbacks and the odds stacked against her, Sarah remained optimistic about her app's potential impact on people's lives. This optimism kept her going.

- Vision: Sarah's unwavering vision of creating a healthier world through technology propelled her forward, guiding *every decision she made.*

*Sarah's journey exemplifies how the entrepreneurial mindset can empower individuals to overcome challenges and create innovative solutions. It's a mindset that enables entrepreneurs to not just survive but thrive in the ever-shifting landscape of entrepreneurship.*

# Chapter 2: Crafting Your Entrepreneurial Vision

In the turbulent world of entrepreneurship, having a clear and compelling vision is like possessing a guiding star in a vast and unpredictable sea. Your vision is the magnetic north that directs your entrepreneurial compass, keeping you on course when the journey becomes challenging. This chapter is all about the art of crafting your entrepreneurial vision, a critical foundation upon which your entire venture will be built.

## The Power of Vision

A well-defined entrepreneurial vision serves as a roadmap for your journey. It provides direction, inspires your team, and shapes every decision and action you take. This vision is not a mere description of your business; it's a vivid depiction of the future you want to create. Let's explore why a strong vision is essential:

### 1. Motivation

Your vision should be your daily motivation. It's the driving force that compels you to work tirelessly, overcome obstacles, and stay committed, even when challenges seem insurmountable.

### 2. Alignment

A clear vision ensures that everyone on your team is moving in the same direction. It aligns your organization's efforts, making collaboration smoother and more effective.

## 3. Decision-Making

When faced with tough choices, your vision serves as a decision-making compass. It helps you weigh options against your long-term goals and make choices that are consistent with your overall mission.

## 4. Inspiration

A compelling vision inspires not only you but also your team and stakeholders. It creates a sense of purpose and excitement, driving innovation and dedication.

### Crafting Your Vision

## 1. Start with Why

Begin by asking yourself why you want to embark on this entrepreneurial journey. What is the deeper purpose behind your venture? Your "why" should extend beyond financial gain. It could be to solve a pressing problem, improve lives, or bring about positive change in your industry or the world.

## 2. Be Specific

A vague vision is like a blurry photograph — it lacks impact. The more specific and detailed your vision is, the easier it becomes to communicate and execute. Describe not only what your business does but also who it serves, how it operates, and what impact it aims to achieve.

### 3. Make It Inspiring

An inspiring vision should resonate with you and your team on an emotional level. It should ignite passion and enthusiasm. Craft a vision statement that not only conveys what you do but also why it matters.

### 4. Keep It Realistic

While your vision should be inspiring, it should also be attainable. Unrealistic goals can lead to frustration and disappointment. Ensure that your vision is ambitious but within the realm of possibility.

### 5. Long-Term Perspective

Your entrepreneurial vision should extend into the future, capturing a long-term perspective. Think about where you want to be in five, ten, or twenty years. What kind of impact do you want your venture to have over time?

### 6. Test and Refine

Share your vision with trusted advisors, mentors, or colleagues. Seek their input and feedback. A well-crafted vision can benefit from diverse perspectives. Be open to refining and revising it as your venture evolves.

## Case Study: SpaceX - Elon Musk's Vision of Space Exploration

To illustrate the power of a visionary entrepreneurial leader, consider the case of SpaceX, founded by Elon Musk. His vision was not merely to create a profitable business but to revolutionize space exploration. Musk's vision included these elements:

- Why: Musk's "why" was to make humanity a multi-planetary species, ensuring the survival of our species by enabling us to live on other planets.

- Specific: He aimed to make space travel accessible and affordable, reducing the cost of space exploration by developing reusable rockets and spacecraft.

- Inspiring: Musk's vision resonated with people's fascination with space and the future. It attracted a team of talented engineers and scientists who shared his passion.

- Realistic: While ambitious, Musk's vision was grounded in technical feasibility. He broke down the vision into practical steps, such as developing the Falcon 1 and Falcon 9 rockets, before progressing to more ambitious projects.

- Long-Term Perspective: SpaceX's vision extended beyond short-term goals. Musk's goal was to facilitate human colonization of Mars, a project that may span decades.

SpaceX's visionary approach has led to groundbreaking achievements in space technology and exploration, and it continues to inspire not only the company's employees but also the world.

### The Vision in Action

Once you've crafted your entrepreneurial vision, the real work begins. Your vision must be more than words on paper; it should permeate every aspect of your venture. Here's how to put your vision into action:

#### 1. Communicate Clearly

Share your vision with your team, investors, and stakeholders. Make sure everyone understands and embraces it. The more effectively you communicate your vision, the more likely it is to become a driving force in your organization.

#### 2. Set Milestones

Break down your long-term vision into manageable milestones. These are smaller, actionable goals that lead you toward your larger objective. Milestones provide a clear path forward and enable you to measure progress.

#### 3. Align Your Strategies

Your business strategies, from product development to marketing, should align with your vision. Ask whether each decision and action advances your mission. If not, reconsider the approach.

### 4. Adapt and Evolve

Your vision may need adjustments as your venture progresses and the market evolves. Be open to revisiting and refining your vision statement to ensure it remains relevant and inspiring.

### 5. Lead by Example

As an entrepreneurial leader, embody your vision in your actions and decisions. Show your dedication to your mission, and your team will follow suit.

## Chapter 3: Navigating Risk and Uncertainty

In the unpredictable world of entrepreneurship, risk is your constant companion. The terrain is often uncharted, and the path is riddled with uncertainty. Yet, it's within this very uncertainty that great opportunities lie. This chapter delves into the intricacies of navigating risk and uncertainty as an entrepreneur, exploring strategies to make informed decisions, manage risks, and find your way to success in an ever-shifting landscape.

### Understanding Risk in Entrepreneurship

Risk, in the context of entrepreneurship, is the potential for harm or loss when pursuing an opportunity. It comes in various forms, such as financial risk, operational risk, and market risk. While risk is often associated with negative outcomes, it's essential to recognize that calculated risks can lead to significant rewards.

### 1. Calculated Risks

Calculated risks are those that are taken with careful consideration and analysis. They involve a degree of uncertainty but are based on a rational assessment of potential benefits. Successful entrepreneurs understand that risk is an inherent part of the entrepreneurial journey and are willing to take calculated risks to achieve their goals.

## 2. Risk Tolerance

Every entrepreneur has a unique risk tolerance. Some are more risk-averse and prefer to minimize exposure, while others are risk-tolerant, willing to take significant gambles. Understanding your own risk tolerance is crucial, as it influences your decision-making and your approach to risk management.

## 3. Risk versus Reward

In entrepreneurship, risk and reward are often closely linked. The potential for higher rewards typically accompanies higher risks. Entrepreneurs weigh the potential benefits against the potential downsides when deciding to pursue an opportunity or take a specific course of action.

## Strategies for Managing Uncertainty

While risk is a fundamental aspect of entrepreneurship, managing uncertainty is equally crucial. Here are some strategies to navigate the turbulent waters of unpredictability:

## 1. Scenario Planning

Scenario planning involves developing multiple scenarios for potential future outcomes. By considering a range of possibilities, entrepreneurs can better prepare for various situations. This approach reduces the element of surprise and allows for more agile decision-making.

## 2. Risk Mitigation

Risk mitigation involves taking steps to reduce the impact of potential risks. This can include diversifying revenue sources, setting up contingency plans, and implementing safeguards to minimize the consequences of adverse events.

## 3. Continuous Learning

Entrepreneurs should be committed to ongoing learning and adaptability. Staying informed about industry trends, market shifts, and emerging technologies is essential. This knowledge helps entrepreneurs anticipate and respond to changes effectively.

### 4. Access to Expertise

Seeking advice from mentors, advisors, and industry experts can provide valuable insights. These individuals can offer guidance on risk assessment and suggest strategies for managing specific challenges.

### 5. Data-Driven Decision-Making

Data can be a powerful tool for risk assessment and decision-making. Entrepreneurs should gather and analyze relevant data to inform their choices. By relying on data, they can make more informed and rational decisions.

## Balancing Risk-Taking

Entrepreneurs must strike a balance between taking risks and managing them. This balance is essential for ensuring that the risks taken align with the overall goals of the venture and do not jeopardize its long-term sustainability.

### 1. Risk Assessment

Before taking a risk, it's vital to assess the potential impact and likelihood of success. Entrepreneurs should ask critical questions such as: What is the potential return on investment? What is the worst-case scenario, and how can it be managed?

## 2. Risk Tolerance

Understanding your own risk tolerance is crucial. Entrepreneurs should be honest with themselves about how much risk they can comfortably handle. It's important not to push beyond your risk tolerance, as this can lead to stress and burnout.

## 3. Risk Diversification

Diversifying risks involves spreading risk across different areas of the business. This can include offering a range of products or services, targeting multiple customer segments, or entering various markets. Diversification can help mitigate the impact of individual failures.

### Case Study: Airbnb's Risky Expansion

Airbnb, the global online marketplace for lodging and travel experiences, faced a significant risk when it decided to expand internationally. The company had established a strong presence in the United States and was enjoying rapid growth. However, to achieve its ambitious vision, Airbnb needed to enter international markets, a move that involved substantial risk.

**Risk Assessment:** Airbnb's leadership recognized the potential for regulatory challenges, cultural differences, and the need to build trust among both hosts and guests in new countries. Despite these challenges, the potential reward of becoming a global leader in the travel industry was compelling.

**Risk Mitigation:** Airbnb implemented a range of risk mitigation strategies. It sought local partners to navigate regulatory complexities, adapted its platform to cater to international preferences, and invested in localized marketing and customer support.

**Success:** Airbnb's calculated risk paid off, leading to significant global expansion and becoming a household name in the travel industry. The company's ability to balance risk-taking with effective risk management has been a key factor in its success.

### Decision-Making Under Uncertainty

Entrepreneurs often face choices in uncertain environments. Effective decision-making under uncertainty involves the following steps:

#### 1. Define the Problem

Clearly articulate the problem or decision you're facing. Ensure that everyone involved understands the issue at hand.

#### 2. Gather Information

Collect relevant data and information that can help inform your decision. This might include market research, customer feedback, and industry trends.

#### 3. Generate Options

Brainstorm potential solutions or courses of action. Encourage creativity and consider a range of possibilities.

#### 4. Evaluate Risks and Benefits

Assess the potential risks and benefits associated with each option. Consider the likelihood of success and the potential impact on your business.

### 5. Make the Decision

Once you've weighed the options, make a decision and take action. Avoid analysis paralysis, but ensure that your choice is well-informed.

### 6. Monitor and Adapt

Continuously monitor the results of your decision. Be prepared to adapt and make course corrections as needed.

## Chapter 4: Building Your Dream Team

In the entrepreneurial landscape, success is rarely a solo endeavor. Instead, it's a collective achievement, built on the foundation of a skilled and cohesive team. This chapter explores the crucial role of assembling, managing, and leading your dream team as an entrepreneur. It delves into the qualities that define a high-performing team, effective leadership strategies, and the culture that fuels innovation and adaptability.

### The Power of a Dream Team

Entrepreneurs are the visionaries and strategists behind their ventures, but it's the team they surround themselves with that breathes life into those visions. A dream team is not just a group of individuals working together; it's a harmonious ensemble of diverse talents and skills, all aligned with a common purpose.

### 1. Diverse Expertise

A dream team comprises individuals with a range of expertise. They bring different skills, perspectives, and experiences to the table, allowing the team to tackle a broader spectrum of challenges.

## 2. Collaborative Spirit

Members of a dream team work cohesively, valuing open communication and cooperation. They understand the importance of sharing ideas, supporting one another, and collectively pursuing the venture's goals.

## 3. Shared Vision

A shared vision unites the team, ensuring that everyone is working toward the same goals. This shared understanding fosters alignment and commitment, making the pursuit of those goals more effective.

## 4. Commitment

Each team member is deeply committed to the venture's success. They are willing to put in the effort and time required to achieve the shared vision, even when faced with challenges.

## 5. Adaptability

In the dynamic world of entrepreneurship, adaptability is essential. A dream team is flexible and capable of adjusting to changing circumstances and learning from setbacks.

### Building Your Dream Team

Assembling your dream team is a pivotal task. It's not just about hiring the most skilled individuals but also ensuring that the team's dynamics are conducive to success. Here's how to go about it:

1. Define Your Needs

Start by identifying the specific roles and skill sets required for your venture. Determine the expertise, experience, and traits that will complement your vision and business strategy.

2. Cast a Wide Net

Seek talent from diverse sources. This includes recruiting from various backgrounds, industries, and demographics. A broad talent pool can bring fresh perspectives and innovative solutions to your team.

3. Assess Cultural Fit

While skills and expertise are essential, cultural fit should not be underestimated. Ensure that potential team members share your values, work ethic, and vision. A strong cultural fit fosters a more harmonious work environment.

## 4. Leverage Networks

Leverage your personal and professional networks to identify potential team members. Recommendations from trusted contacts can lead to finding individuals who align with your vision and values.

## 5. Evaluate Soft Skills

In addition to technical skills, evaluate soft skills such as communication, adaptability, and problem-solving abilities. These skills contribute to effective teamwork and collaboration.

## 6. Set High Expectations

When recruiting, set high expectations for potential team members. Encourage them to rise to the challenge and share your commitment to achieving the venture's goals.

### Effective Leadership in Team Building

As an entrepreneur, you're not just a business owner; you're a leader. Effective leadership is essential for building and guiding a high-performing team. It involves the following key aspects:

## 1. Visionary Leadership

Articulate a clear and compelling vision for your team. A visionary leader inspires others by outlining the future they aim to create together.

## 2. Lead by Example

Demonstrate the work ethic, commitment, and values you expect from your team. Leading by example sets the standard for your organization.

## 3. Communicate Effectively

Open and transparent communication is a cornerstone of effective leadership. Keep your team informed about the venture's goals, progress, and any challenges that may arise.

## 4. Delegate Responsibilities

Avoid micromanagement by delegating responsibilities to team members. Trust their expertise and provide them with the autonomy to execute their tasks.

## 5. Provide Feedback

Regularly provide constructive feedback to help team members grow and improve. Celebrate their successes and address areas for development.

## 6. Foster Innovation

Encourage innovation and creativity within your team. Create an environment where team members feel comfortable sharing new ideas and taking calculated risks.

## 7. Resolve Conflict

Conflict can arise within any team. Effective leaders address conflicts promptly and constructively, seeking resolutions that benefit the team's cohesion.

## Nurturing a Culture of Innovation and Adaptability

Innovation and adaptability are at the heart of entrepreneurial success. Fostering a culture that nurtures these qualities can set your team on the path to continuous growth and achievement.

## 1. Encourage Experimentation

Create a safe space for team members to experiment and take risks. Encourage them to explore new ideas, even if they might lead to failure.

## 2. Embrace Continuous Learning

Cultivate a culture of lifelong learning. Provide opportunities for team members to expand their skills and knowledge, both inside and outside their roles.

## 3. Celebrate Successes and Failures

Acknowledge and celebrate successes, no matter how small. Likewise, view failures as learning opportunities and celebrate the lessons gained from them.

## 4. Promote Agility

In a rapidly changing world, agility is key. Encourage your team to adapt to new circumstances and pivot when necessary. The ability to change direction swiftly can be a competitive advantage.

## 5. Lead with a Growth Mindset

A growth mindset, as popularized by psychologist Carol Dweck, is the belief that abilities and intelligence can be developed with effort and learning. Encourage your team to adopt a growth mindset, fostering resilience and a willingness to learn.

## Case Study: Google's Innovative Culture

Google is renowned for its innovative culture, which has been instrumental in its success as a tech giant. Key elements of Google's culture include:

1. Freedom to Innovate: Google encourages its employees to devote a portion of their work hours to personal projects. This freedom to innovate has led to groundbreaking products, including Gmail and Google News.

2. Fail Fast, Learn Fast: Google embraces a culture of experimentation and acknowledges that not all ideas will succeed. The company encourages employees to take risks and learn from their failures.

3. Collaboration: Google promotes a collaborative environment where employees across different departments and functions are encouraged to share ideas and insights. Cross-functional collaboration often leads to innovative solutions.

4. Employee Development: Google invests in employee development through various programs, including ongoing training and access to educational resources. This commitment to learning fosters a culture of adaptability.

5. Visionary Leadership: The company's founders, Larry Page and Sergey Brin, have provided visionary leadership by setting ambitious goals and driving a culture of innovation from the top down.

## Chapter 5: Creating Value in Chaos

In the dynamic world of entrepreneurship, chaos is a constant companion. Markets evolve, technologies advance, and customer needs change rapidly. Yet, within this chaos lies a world of opportunity for those who can identify and create value in the midst of disruption. This chapter explores the art of developing innovative products and services, strategies for identifying customer needs and solving their problems, and how to leverage disruption as an opportunity for growth.

### The Entrepreneurial Imperative: Innovation

Innovation is the lifeblood of entrepreneurship. It's the process of creating new or improved products, services, processes, or business models that provide unique value to customers. Innovation is not just about generating ideas; it's about executing those ideas to drive real, tangible value. Here's why innovation is crucial:

### 1. Staying Relevant

In a rapidly changing world, businesses that fail to innovate risk becoming obsolete. Customers expect fresh solutions that address their evolving needs and preferences.

## 2. Competitive Advantage

Innovation can set your business apart from competitors. Unique products or services can capture market share and establish your brand as a leader.

## 3. Growth and Expansion

Innovative solutions open doors to new markets and revenue streams. By solving unmet needs, you can fuel business growth.

## 4. Problem Solving

Innovation is often about identifying and addressing customer pain points. By solving problems effectively, you can build strong customer loyalty.

### Developing Innovative Products and Services

Innovative products and services are born from a deep understanding of your target audience and their needs. Here's a systematic approach to developing innovation:

## 1. Customer-Centric Approach

Begin by understanding your target customers. What are their pain points, unmet needs, and desires? Conduct surveys, interviews, and market research to gather insights.

## 2. Ideation

Encourage your team to brainstorm creative ideas. Embrace diverse perspectives and foster an environment where innovative thinking is valued. Ideation sessions can yield a range of concepts.

## 3. Validation

Not all ideas will translate into successful innovations. Validate your concepts with customers, getting their feedback on whether the proposed solution resonates with their needs.

## 4. Prototyping

Create prototypes or minimum viable products (MVPs) to test the concept in a real-world context. Prototyping allows you to gather more insights and refine the solution.

## 5. Iteration

Based on feedback and testing, iterate on the concept. Make improvements and refinements to enhance the product or service.

## 6. Scalability

Consider how the innovation can scale to meet a larger market. Scalability is essential for capturing significant market share.

## 7. Launch and Marketing

When the product or service is ready, launch it effectively. Develop a marketing strategy that highlights the unique value and benefits it offers.

## Identifying Customer Needs and Problem Solving

To create value in chaos, you must identify and address customer needs effectively. Here's how to do it:

## 1. Listen Actively

Pay close attention to your customers. Listen to their feedback, reviews, and suggestions. Customer insights are a goldmine of information about their needs and pain points.

## 2. Data Analysis

Leverage data analytics to gain deeper insights into customer behavior and preferences. Analyzing data can reveal patterns and trends that inform your innovation.

### 3. Problem Validation

Don't assume you know your customers' problems. Validate them by engaging with customers directly. Ask questions, conduct surveys, and explore their pain points in-depth.

### 4. Co-Creation

Involve customers in the co-creation process. Collaborative innovation can lead to solutions that precisely match customer needs.

### 5. Feedback Loops

Establish feedback loops to continuously gather customer input. Use this feedback to refine your products and services over time.

### 6. Test and Learn

Implement a test-and-learn approach. Launch small-scale experiments to assess the viability of new concepts. Learn from the results and adapt accordingly.

### Leveraging Disruption as an Opportunity

Disruption, in the entrepreneurial context, refers to significant shifts in markets, technologies, or customer behaviors that challenge existing business models. While disruption can be unsettling, it also presents opportunities for growth. Here's how to leverage disruption as a catalyst for success:

### 1. Anticipate Disruption

Monitor your industry and market for signs of disruption. Anticipating change allows you to prepare and adapt proactively.

### 2. Embrace Change

Rather than resisting disruption, embrace it. Be willing to adapt and pivot your business model in response to new circumstances.

### 3. Innovate Continuously

Use disruption as a driver for innovation. Disruptive forces can lead to the creation of groundbreaking products and services that cater to emerging needs.

### 4. Agility and Flexibility

Cultivate organizational agility and flexibility. Ensure

that your business can pivot quickly and adjust to new market dynamics.

## Case Study: Netflix - Transforming the Entertainment Industry

Netflix, a leading streaming service, exemplifies the power of innovation and disruption in transforming an industry. Netflix began as a DVD rental service but swiftly embraced digital streaming, significantly disrupting the traditional television and film industry. Key elements of Netflix's success include:

1. Customer Insights: Netflix paid close attention to customer behavior and preferences. It recognized the changing way people consume entertainment.

2. Digital Streaming: The company quickly transitioned from DVDs to digital streaming, catering to the evolving needs of viewers. It also invested in producing original content, which further disrupted the industry.

3. Data Analytics: Netflix heavily leveraged data analytics to understand user behavior and create personalized recommendations, enhancing the user experience.

4. Global Expansion: Netflix expanded internationally,

tapping into a global market and becoming a dominant force in the streaming industry.

Netflix's innovative approach and adaptability in the face of industry disruption allowed it to revolutionize how people access and consume entertainment.

## Chapter 6: Financing Your Venture

In the entrepreneurial world, the fuel that drives innovation and growth is capital. Securing the right financing for your venture is a critical aspect of entrepreneurial success. This chapter delves into the exploration of various funding options for startups, the importance of financial planning and management, and strategies for navigating cash flow challenges and allocating capital effectively.

### The Lifeblood of Entrepreneurship: Capital

Capital is the lifeblood of entrepreneurship. It's the financial resource that fuels the creation and growth of startups. Whether you're launching a new venture or scaling an existing one, securing the right funding is essential. Here's why capital is crucial:

1. Fueling Innovation

Capital enables you to invest in research, development, and innovation. It allows you to create and improve products and services.

2. Scaling Operations

As your venture grows, you need capital to expand operations, hire talent, and reach new markets. Scaling requires financial resources.

### 3. Mitigating Risk

Having access to capital provides a safety net. It helps you weather unexpected challenges and market fluctuations.

### 4. Seizing Opportunities

Capital allows you to seize time-sensitive opportunities. Whether it's acquiring a competitor or entering a new market, having the funds available is essential.

## Funding Options for Startups

There is no one-size-fits-all approach to funding a startup. Different ventures have unique financial needs and may seek capital from various sources. Here are some of the primary funding options for startups:

### 1. Bootstrapping

Bootstrapping involves self-funding your venture, typically using personal savings, revenue from the business, or loans from family and friends. It provides complete control but may limit the scale of your operations.

## 2. Angel Investors

Angel investors are high-net-worth individuals who provide capital in exchange for equity in the company. They often offer not only funding but also valuable mentorship and connections.

## 3. Venture Capital

Venture capital firms invest in startups with high growth potential. They typically provide larger sums of capital in exchange for equity. Venture capitalists often take an active role in guiding the company.

## 4. Crowdfunding

Crowdfunding platforms allow startups to raise funds from a large number of individuals. It's a way to secure capital while also building a community of supporters.

## 5. Small Business Loans

Entrepreneurs can apply for loans from banks or other financial institutions. These loans provide capital but come with the obligation to repay with interest.

### 6. Grants and Competitions

Various organizations and government agencies offer grants and prizes to innovative startups. These non-dilutive funding sources do not require giving up equity.

### 7. Corporate Partnerships

Establishing partnerships with established companies can provide both capital and access to resources, expertise, and markets.

### 8. Initial Coin Offerings (ICOs)

In the world of blockchain and cryptocurrencies, ICOs allow startups to raise capital by issuing tokens or coins. This is a unique form of fundraising.

### 9. Self-Financing

Some entrepreneurs rely on their personal savings, assets, or income to fund their ventures entirely. This approach provides full ownership but carries personal financial risk.

The choice of funding option depends on your venture's stage, goals, and financial requirements. It's essential to evaluate which source aligns best with your business model and vision.

### Financial Planning and Management

Sound financial planning and management are the cornerstones of successful entrepreneurship. It's not just about securing funds; it's about using them effectively and efficiently. Here are key elements to consider:

### 1. Budgeting

Create a detailed budget that outlines your expected expenses and revenue. Budgets serve as roadmaps, helping you track financial performance and make informed decisions.

### 2. Cash Flow Management

Cash flow management is crucial. Monitor your cash inflow and outflow to ensure that you can cover expenses and seize opportunities when they arise.

### 3. Contingency Planning

Always have contingency plans in place. Consider potential financial challenges and develop strategies for mitigating their impact.

## 4. Financial Forecasting

Create financial forecasts that extend into the future. These projections help you plan for growth, investment, and financial stability.

## 5. Cost Management

Efficiently manage costs and expenses. Look for opportunities to reduce overhead while maintaining or improving quality.

## 6. Record-Keeping

Maintain accurate and detailed financial records. Effective record-keeping is essential for compliance, taxes, and strategic planning.

## 7. Tax Strategy

Develop a tax strategy to minimize tax liabilities while remaining compliant with tax laws. Tax planning can significantly impact your bottom line.

### Navigating Cash Flow Challenges

Cash flow challenges are a common hurdle for startups. Even with a solid business plan, you may encounter periods of financial strain. Here's how to navigate cash flow challenges effectively:

### 1. Build a Cash Reserve

Before launching or scaling, build a cash reserve to cover operational costs during lean times. Having a buffer can provide peace of mind.

### 2. Monitor Receivables and Payables

Keep a close eye on accounts receivable (money owed to your business) and accounts payables (money you owe). Managing these effectively can help maintain a healthy cash flow.

### 3. Revise Payment Terms

Consider adjusting payment terms with suppliers and customers to align with your cash flow needs. Negotiate favorable terms that support your financial stability.

### 4. Seek Short-Term Financing

Short-term financing options, such as lines of credit or short-term loans, can provide temporary relief during cash flow challenges.

### 5. Cut Non-Essential Costs

Identify and reduce non-essential costs during challenging periods. Streamlining operations can free up cash for critical expenses.

## 6. Explore Invoice Financing

Invoice financing allows you to receive immediate cash for outstanding invoices. It's a solution to bridge the gap between invoicing and payment.

## 7. Maintain Communication

Maintain open communication with suppliers, lenders, and investors. They may be willing to work with you during challenging times if they understand the situation.

### Allocating Capital Effectively

Securing capital is one thing; using it wisely is another. Effective capital allocation is essential for sustainable growth. Here are strategies for allocating capital effectively:

### 1. Prioritize Investment

Identify the areas of your business that require investment for growth. Allocate capital to initiatives that will have the most significant impact on your venture.

## 2. Diversify Investments

Avoid putting all your capital into a single project or initiative. Diversifying investments can help spread risk and increase the likelihood of success.

## 3. Measure ROI

Continuously measure the return on investment (ROI) for your capital allocations. Make data-driven decisions about where to invest for the best outcomes.

## 4. Reinvest in the Business

Consider reinvesting profits back into the business. This can help fund future growth and innovation.

## 5. Emergency Fund

Set aside a portion of capital as an emergency fund to cover unexpected expenses or opportunities.

## 6. Focus on Growth

Allocate capital to initiatives that drive growth and expand your customer base. Growth-focused investments can provide the most substantial returns.

## 7. Monitor and Adjust

Regularly monitor the performance of capital allocations. Be prepared to adjust your strategy based on results and changing market conditions.

### Case Study: SpaceX - Leveraging Funding for Innovation

SpaceX, the private aerospace manufacturer and space transportation company founded by Elon Musk, is a remarkable example of how innovative startups can leverage various sources of funding to achieve groundbreaking innovation. SpaceX aimed to revolutionize space travel and make it more cost-effective, with a long-term vision of making life multi-planetary. Key elements of SpaceX's funding and innovation strategy include:

1. Visionary Leadership: Elon Musk's clear vision for the future of space travel and his commitment to achieving it inspired investors and supporters.

2. Government Contracts: SpaceX secured contracts with NASA to supply the International Space Station. This provided both funding and credibility to the company.

3. Private Investment: Musk and other private investors poured significant capital into the company, believing in the potential for disrupting the space industry.

4. Reusable Rockets: SpaceX's groundbreaking achievement of developing reusable rockets dramatically lowered the cost of space travel and attracted more customers.

5. Commercial Launches: SpaceX expanded its revenue streams by providing commercial satellite launches, further solidifying its financial stability.

6. Starship Project: SpaceX is continually investing in its Starship project, aiming to make interplanetary travel a reality.

SpaceX's ability to secure funding from various sources, its focus on innovation, and its commitment to long-term goals illustrate the power of effective capital allocation and financial planning in the pursuit of ambitious entrepreneurial ventures.

# Chapter 7: Marketing in Dynamic Environments

In the ever-evolving world of entrepreneurship, marketing is the bridge that connects your venture with the ever-shifting landscape of consumer behavior, competition, and technology. This chapter explores the art of building a brand and marketing strategy in fluid markets, the power of leveraging digital marketing, social media, and emerging trends, and the strategies for building and maintaining lasting customer relationships in turbulent times.

## The Art of Adaptable Marketing

Marketing in dynamic environments requires a different approach than traditional marketing. Instead of rigid plans, it's about adaptability and responsiveness. Here's why adaptable marketing is essential:

### 1. Changing Customer Behavior

Consumer behavior evolves rapidly, especially in the digital age. What worked yesterday might not work today. To stay relevant, you must continuously adapt.

## 2. Fluid Competition

Competition in the entrepreneurial landscape is dynamic. New players emerge, and established ones pivot and evolve. Adaptable marketing is necessary to compete effectively.

## 3. Technological Advances

The pace of technological change impacts marketing. Leveraging emerging technologies can give you a competitive edge.

## 4. Unpredictable Markets

Markets can be unpredictable, subject to economic shifts, global events, and trends. Adaptable marketing allows you to react to market changes swiftly.

## Building a Resilient Brand

A resilient brand is one that can withstand challenges and adapt to changing environments. Here's how to build a brand that thrives in dynamic markets:

## 1. Clarity of Purpose

Clearly define your brand's purpose and values. This

clarity guides your marketing efforts and resonates with consumers who share your vision.

## 2. Consistency

Maintain consistency in branding across all touchpoints, from your website to social media profiles and customer interactions. Consistency builds trust.

## 3. Adaptability

Be willing to adapt and evolve. Your brand identity should remain flexible enough to respond to market shifts and customer feedback.

## 4. Storytelling

Effective storytelling can help consumers connect with your brand on a deeper level. Share your journey, values, and impact through compelling narratives.

## 5. Personalization

Tailor your brand's messaging to individual customer segments. Personalization enhances engagement and relevance.

### Building a Dynamic Marketing Strategy

A dynamic marketing strategy is one that can shift and evolve based on market conditions and consumer behavior. Here's how to build such a strategy:

### 1. Market Research

Regularly conduct market research to stay updated on consumer trends, competitive landscapes, and emerging opportunities.

### 2. Data-Driven Insights

Leverage data analytics to gain insights into customer behavior. This data can inform your marketing decisions and strategies.

### 3. Agile Planning

Adopt agile marketing practices, allowing you to respond quickly to market changes. Develop a strategy that can be adjusted on the fly.

### 4. Emerging Platforms

Explore emerging marketing platforms and trends. Experimenting with new channels can help you reach new audiences.

### 5. Customer Feedback

Listen to your customers. Their feedback is a valuable source of information on how to improve your products and marketing efforts.

## The Power of Digital Marketing

Digital marketing has become a cornerstone of modern entrepreneurship. It offers cost-effective ways to reach a global audience. Here's why digital marketing is a powerful tool:

### 1. Global Reach

Digital marketing allows you to reach a global audience. With the right strategies, your venture can expand beyond borders.

### 2. Cost-Effective

Compared to traditional advertising, digital marketing is often more cost-effective. It offers a high return on investment (ROI).

### 3. Targeted Marketing

Digital marketing enables precise targeting. You can tailor your marketing efforts to reach specific demographics and customer segments.

### 4. Real-Time Feedback

Digital marketing provides real-time data and feedback. You can monitor the performance of your campaigns and adjust them as needed.

### 5. Diverse Channels

There are numerous digital marketing channels, from social media and email marketing to content marketing and search engine optimization. Diversifying your efforts can increase your reach.

### The Role of Social Media

Social media has revolutionized marketing. It's a powerful tool for building brand awareness, engaging with customers, and staying updated on industry trends. Here's how to leverage social media effectively:

### 1. Choose the Right Platforms

Not all social media platforms are suitable for every venture. Select the platforms that align with your target audience and marketing goals.

### 2. Engage with Your Audience

Engagement is crucial on social media. Respond to

comments, engage in conversations, and build relationships with your followers.

### 3. Content Strategy

Develop a content strategy that provides value to your audience. Create and share content that resonates with your brand's purpose and customer interests.

### 4. Visual Storytelling

Visual content, such as images and videos, can be highly engaging on social media. Use visual storytelling to convey your brand's message.

### 5. Monitor Trends

Stay updated on social media trends and changes. What works on social media evolves, and adapting to these shifts is essential for success.

### Nurturing Customer Relationships

Building lasting customer relationships is fundamental for entrepreneurial success. Here's how to foster relationships that stand the test of time:

### 1. Personalization

Tailor your interactions to individual customers. Personalization makes customers feel valued and understood.

### 2. Communication

Maintain open lines of communication with your customers. Listen to their feedback, answer their questions, and address their concerns.

### 3. Loyalty Programs

Implement loyalty programs and rewards to incentivize repeat business. Loyalty programs create a sense of belonging and appreciation.

### 4. Surveys and Feedback

Gather customer feedback through surveys and reviews. Use this feedback to enhance your products and services.

### 5. Consistency

Consistency in quality and service is vital for building trust. Customers should know what to expect from your venture.

## Case Study: Airbnb - Leveraging Dynamic Marketing and Customer Relationships

Airbnb, a global online marketplace for lodging and travel experiences, exemplifies the power of dynamic marketing and strong customer relationships. Key elements of Airbnb's success include:

1. Dynamic Marketing: Airbnb leverages various digital marketing channels, including social media and content marketing, to reach a global audience. The company's marketing strategies adapt to different markets and customer segments.

2. User-Generated Content: Airbnb encourages users to share their experiences and stories. This user-generated content serves as a powerful marketing tool, building trust and engagement.

3. Community Building: Airbnb has nurtured a community of hosts and guests. By fostering a sense of belonging and shared values, the company strengthens customer relationships.

4. Personalization: Airbnb provides personalized recommendations and search results, tailoring the user experience to individual preferences.

5.Adaptability and Innovation: Airbnb continuously innovates and adapts to emerging trends. For example, the company expanded its services to include experiences and boutique stays, addressing changing customer demands.

Airbnb's success story highlights the importance of agile marketing strategies and nurturing strong customer relationships. By embracing change, leveraging user-generated content, and personalizing the user experience, Airbnb has become a leading platform in the travel and accommodation industry.

## Chapter 8: Scaling Your Success

Scaling your venture is the ultimate aspiration for most entrepreneurs. It's the journey from startup to a thriving, sustainable business. However, the path to scaling is fraught with challenges and opportunities. In this chapter, we'll explore strategies for scaling your business while preserving your core values, managing growth, scalability, and ongoing innovation, and preparing for new challenges as your venture expands.

### The Scaling Imperative

Scaling your business is about more than just making it bigger. It's about optimizing growth and efficiency while staying true to your mission and values. Here's why scaling is crucial:

1. Efficient Resource Utilization

Scaling allows you to make more efficient use of resources, both in terms of time and capital. You can reach more customers, provide more value, and increase profitability.

2. Market Expansion

Scaling often involves entering new markets or demographics. This diversification helps reduce risk and enhances long-term stability.

### 3. Competitive Advantage

A well-executed scaling strategy can position your business as a dominant player in your industry. It enables you to outpace competitors and capture market share.

### 4. Innovation and Evolution

Scaling encourages ongoing innovation and evolution within your venture. As you expand, you're likely to develop new products, services, and processes.

### Preserving Core Values

As your venture grows, it's essential to preserve the core values that define your brand. Here's how to do it:

### 1. Define Core Values

Start by clearly defining your core values. What principles guide your business? What beliefs are non-negotiable?

## 2. Cultural Alignment

Ensure that your team and employees align with these values. Foster a culture that reflects your core principles.

## 3. Communicate Values

Consistently communicate your values to both your team and your customers. Transparency builds trust and reinforces your brand identity.

## 4. Make Values Non-Negotiable

In decision-making, make your core values non-negotiable. Uphold them even when facing difficult choices.

## 5. Accountability

Hold yourself and your team accountable for living the company's core values. Regularly review and assess your adherence to them.

## Managing Growth and Scalability

Scaling involves more than just adding customers or expanding product lines. It requires a strategic approach to managing growth. Here's how to do it effectively:

## 1. Scalable Business Model

Your business model should be inherently scalable. It must support growth without causing significant disruptions.

## 2. Systems and Processes

Develop and optimize systems and processes that can handle increased demand. Automation and efficient workflows are key.

## 3. Talent Acquisition

Hiring the right talent is crucial. Ensure that you have the expertise and human resources needed to sustain growth.

## 4. Financial Management

Maintain a focus on financial management. Scalability should not come at the cost of fiscal responsibility.

## 5. Data-Driven Decision-Making

Leverage data to drive decision-making. Data analysis can reveal areas for improvement and opportunities for growth.

### Ongoing Innovation

Innovation doesn't stop once you've achieved some level of success. It's a continual process that must be woven into your scaling strategy. Here's how to foster ongoing innovation:

### 1. Create an Innovation Culture

Cultivate a culture that encourages and rewards innovation. Empower your team to think creatively and experiment.

### 2. Customer-Centric Innovation

Innovate with a focus on your customers. Understand their evolving needs and desires and develop solutions to meet them.

### 3. Iterate and Experiment

Embrace a culture of iteration and experimentation. Not every idea will succeed, but each failure is an opportunity to learn and improve.

### 4. Invest in Research and Development

Allocate resources to research and development efforts. This investment can lead to breakthrough innovations that drive growth.

### 5. Stay Updated on Trends

Stay updated on industry trends and emerging technologies. Being aware of changes in your market can inform your innovation strategy.

### Preparing for New Challenges

As your venture scales, new challenges will inevitably arise. Anticipating and preparing for these challenges is essential. Here are some common challenges and strategies to address them:

### 1. Market Saturation

In a mature market, competition can become fierce. To address this, focus on differentiation, innovation, and customer retention.

### 2. Operational Complexity

As your business grows, operations can become more complex. Implement efficient systems and streamline processes to maintain control.

### 3. Talent Management

Managing a growing team can be a challenge. Invest in leadership and management development to ensure that your team remains cohesive and productive.

### 4. Financial Sustainability

Scaling requires capital, and financial sustainability is a concern. Plan for capital needs in advance, and consider diverse funding options.

### 5. Customer Retention

Expanding your customer base is important, but don't neglect existing customers. A focus on retention can provide stability and consistent revenue.

### Case Study: Amazon - Mastering Scalability

Amazon, the global e-commerce and technology giant, is a prime example of a company that has mastered scalability. Key elements of Amazon's success in scaling include:

1. Customer-Centric Approach: Amazon's relentless focus on customer satisfaction has been a driving force behind its growth. The company continually seeks ways to improve the customer experience.

2. Innovation Culture: Amazon nurtures a culture of innovation. The company has expanded beyond e-commerce to include cloud computing services (Amazon Web Services), artificial intelligence (Alexa),

and more. This diversification illustrates Amazon's commitment to ongoing innovation.

3. Logistics and Fulfillment: Amazon has invested heavily in building a robust logistics and fulfillment network. This infrastructure supports the rapid delivery of products and services, even as the company continues to grow.

4. Global Expansion: Amazon expanded globally, reaching customers in numerous countries. This global reach has allowed the company to tap into a diverse range of markets.

5. Acquisition Strategy: Amazon has strategically acquired companies that complement its core offerings. For example, the acquisition of Whole Foods expanded its presence in the grocery market.

Amazon's journey from an online bookstore to a global e-commerce and technology giant demonstrates the power of a customer-centric approach, ongoing innovation, and strategic acquisitions in achieving scalability.

## Chapter 9: Embracing Failure and Learning

In the entrepreneurial journey, setbacks and failures are not detours but essential milestones on the path to success. This chapter explores the transformative power of embracing failures as valuable learning experiences, building a culture of continuous improvement within your organization, and the crucial role of resilience in facing adversity.

### The Wisdom in Failure

Failure is an intrinsic part of entrepreneurship. In fact, it's often through setbacks and failures that entrepreneurs find their greatest opportunities for growth and success. Here's why embracing failure is crucial:

1. Valuable Learning

Failures provide invaluable lessons that can't be obtained through success alone. They reveal weaknesses, inefficiencies, and areas for improvement.

2. Innovation Catalyst

Many innovations and breakthroughs stem from failed attempts. By learning from what went wrong, you can develop more creative and effective solutions.

### 3. Resilience Building

Overcoming failures and setbacks builds resilience. It fosters the mental and emotional strength needed to navigate the challenges of entrepreneurship.

### 4. Perseverance

Failure can be a test of your determination and perseverance. It separates those who give up from those who press on toward their goals.

### 5. Continuous Improvement

Failure is a catalyst for continuous improvement. It encourages an ongoing process of refinement and optimization.

### Learning from Failure

To make the most of failures, it's essential to adopt a growth mindset and learn from them. Here's how to do it effectively:

### 1. Reflect

After a setback, take time to reflect on what went wrong. What were the contributing factors, and what can be learned from the experience?

## 2. Identify Root Causes

Dig deeper to identify the root causes of the failure. Was it a flawed strategy, inadequate resources, or external factors beyond your control?

## 3. Adjust and Adapt

Use the insights gained from failure to adjust your approach. Develop a new plan that accounts for the lessons learned.

## 4. Seek Feedback

Engage with mentors, advisors, and team members for feedback. Different perspectives can provide valuable insights.

## 5. Stay Resilient

Acknowledge the emotional impact of failure, but don't let it deter you. Stay resilient and maintain a positive outlook.

## Building a Culture of Continuous Improvement

A culture of continuous improvement is one where learning from failures is not only accepted but encouraged. It's a culture that values growth and progress over perfection. Here's how to foster such a culture within your organization:

## 1. Leadership Example

Leaders set the tone for the entire organization. Demonstrate a commitment to learning and improvement, and your team will follow suit.

## 2. Open Communication

Create an environment where open communication is valued. Encourage team members to share their insights and experiences, both positive and negative.

## 3. Knowledge Sharing

Implement knowledge-sharing practices, such as post-project reviews and regular team meetings to discuss lessons learned.

## 4. Training and Development

Invest in training and development opportunities for your team. Provide them with the skills and knowledge needed to succeed.

## 5. Celebrate Small Wins

Acknowledge and celebrate small victories along the way. Recognize the effort and resilience that lead to progress.

### The Crucial Role of Resilience

Resilience is the ability to bounce back from adversity and setbacks. It's a critical attribute for entrepreneurs facing the challenges of building a business. Here's why resilience is crucial:

1. Coping with Stress

Entrepreneurship is inherently stressful. Resilience helps you cope with the pressures and uncertainties of the journey.

2. Adaptability

Resilience enables you to adapt to changing circumstances and pivot when necessary. It's the flexibility needed in the face of adversity.

3. Maintaining Focus

Resilience keeps you focused on your long-term goals, even when faced with short-term setbacks or distractions.

## 4. Emotional Strength

Entrepreneurship can be emotionally taxing. Resilience provides the emotional strength to keep going, even when things get tough.

## 5. Problem Solving

Resilient individuals are better problem solvers. They look for solutions rather than dwelling on problems.

### Nurturing Resilience

Resilience can be cultivated and strengthened over time. Here's how to nurture resilience in yourself and within your organization:

## 1. Self-Care

Prioritize self-care to maintain physical and mental well-being. This includes exercise, proper nutrition, and relaxation.

## 2. Positive Thinking

Cultivate a positive mindset. Focus on solutions rather than dwelling on problems. Maintain an optimistic outlook.

### 3. Social Support

Lean on your support network, which may include friends, family, mentors, or fellow entrepreneurs. Their encouragement can bolster your resilience.

### 4. Adaptability

Develop adaptability as a core skill. Embrace change and learn to pivot when circumstances demand it.

### 5. Goal Setting

Set clear and achievable goals. A sense of purpose and direction can enhance your resilience.

### Case Study: Steve Jobs - Embracing Setbacks and Innovation

Steve Jobs, the co-founder of Apple Inc., is a prime example of an entrepreneur who embraced failures and setbacks as valuable learning experiences. Key elements of Jobs' journey include:

1. Early Setbacks: Steve Jobs faced setbacks early in his career when he was ousted from Apple, the company he co-founded. Instead of giving up, he went on to found NeXT Computer and Pixar Animation Studios.

2. Learning from Failure: During his time away from Apple, Jobs learned important lessons about leadership, innovation, and branding. These experiences shaped his approach when he returned to Apple.

3. Apple's Turnaround: Jobs returned to Apple and played a pivotal role in the company's turnaround. He introduced innovative products like the iMac, iPod, iPhone, and iPad, revolutionizing multiple industries.

4. Perseverance: Jobs' ability to persevere through personal and professional challenges, including health issues, demonstrated his resilience and determination.

5. Embracing Failure: Steve Jobs once famously said, "I didn't see it then, but it turned out that getting fired from Apple was the best thing that could have ever happened to me." This statement reflects his ability to embrace failure as a stepping stone to greater success.

Steve Jobs' entrepreneurial journey exemplifies the transformative power of embracing failures, learning from setbacks, and using them as opportunities for innovation and growth. His story is a testament to the importance of resilience in the face of adversity.

## Chapter 10: Thriving in Uncertain Times

Entrepreneurship has always been a journey through uncertain territory, but in today's world, uncertainty has reached new heights. This chapter explores the art of navigating economic, social, and technological shifts as an entrepreneur, strategies for achieving long-term sustainability and success, and the profound impact of entrepreneurship on society and the broader world.

### The Uncertainty Conundrum

Uncertainty is the new normal for entrepreneurs. Rapid economic, social, and technological shifts have created an environment where the only constant is change. But within this uncertainty lies tremendous opportunity for those who can adapt and thrive. Here's why navigating uncertainty is essential:

### 1. Economic Volatility

Economic conditions are prone to rapid changes, from global financial crises to market disruptions. Entrepreneurs must be prepared to pivot their strategies.

### 2. Social Dynamics

Society is evolving at an unprecedented pace. Changing demographics, cultural shifts, and consumer behaviors all impact the business landscape.

### 3. Technological Advancements

Technology continues to disrupt industries and create new possibilities. Entrepreneurs who harness technology gain a competitive edge.

### 4. Global Connectivity

The world is more connected than ever. Globalization opens new markets but also increases competition.

### 5. Environmental Factors

Environmental concerns, climate change, and sustainability are becoming central considerations for businesses and consumers alike.

### Strategies for Thriving in Uncertainty

Thriving in uncertain times requires a combination of adaptability, innovation, and strategic planning. Here are some strategies to navigate the uncertainty:

### 1. Agile Planning

Embrace agile planning processes that allow you to adjust your strategies quickly in response to changing conditions.

## 2. Risk Management

Develop a robust risk management strategy to assess, mitigate, and prepare for potential challenges.

## 3. Continuous Learning

Cultivate a culture of continuous learning within your organization. Encourage your team to stay updated on industry trends and emerging technologies.

## 4. Diversification

Diversify your revenue streams and customer base to reduce dependence on any one market or product.

## 5. Customer-Centric Approach

Stay closely connected to your customers, gathering feedback and insights to shape your strategies and innovations.

### Achieving Long-Term Sustainability

Surviving in the short term is one thing, but achieving long-term sustainability and success is the ultimate goal. Here's how to set the stage for lasting entrepreneurship:

1. Visionary Leadership

Leaders with a clear and inspiring vision are more likely to steer their ventures through uncertain times.

2. Scalability

Build a scalable business model that can withstand growth and accommodate changes in demand.

3. Financial Prudence

Maintain financial discipline. Ensure you have sufficient capital reserves to weather unexpected storms.

4. Sustainable Practices

Incorporate sustainable and ethical business practices into your operations. Sustainability is an increasing concern for both consumers and investors.

### 5. Adaptability

Entrepreneurs who remain open to change and willing to adapt are better positioned for long-term success.

### Impact on Society and the World

Entrepreneurship is not just about individual success; it has a profound impact on society and the broader world. Here's why entrepreneurship matters:

### 1. Economic Growth

Entrepreneurship fuels economic growth by creating jobs, driving innovation, and contributing to GDP.

### 2. Social Innovation

Entrepreneurs often tackle societal challenges through innovative solutions, from healthcare to education.

### 3. Technological Advancement

Entrepreneurship drives technological advancement, creating new opportunities and shaping the future of industries.

### 4. Global Connectivity

Entrepreneurs can bridge cultural and geographical divides, fostering global understanding and cooperation.

### 5. Environmental Responsibility

Entrepreneurs have the power to address environmental concerns and promote sustainability through their businesses.

### Case Study: Elon Musk - Navigating Uncertainty and Impacting the World

Elon Musk, the entrepreneur behind SpaceX, Tesla, and other groundbreaking ventures, exemplifies the power of navigating uncertainty and making a global impact. Key elements of Musk's entrepreneurial journey include:

1. Visionary Leadership: Musk's vision includes reducing humanity's reliance on fossil fuels (Tesla), colonizing Mars (SpaceX), and developing high-speed transportation (Hyperloop). His leadership inspires both his teams and the broader world.

2. Technological Innovation: Musk's ventures are at

the forefront of technological innovation, from electric vehicles and renewable energy to space exploration.

3. Sustainability: Tesla is leading the way in sustainable transportation and energy solutions, addressing environmental concerns.

4. Global Impact: Musk's ambitions extend beyond business. His vision for space exploration and sustainable energy has the potential to impact the entire world.

Elon Musk's journey underscores the potential for entrepreneurs to not only thrive in uncertain times but also to shape the future of our society and planet.

## Conclusion

*"Cultivating Success in Uncertainty: A Comprehensive Handbook for Entrepreneurs"* is a roadmap through the ever-shifting terrain of entrepreneurship. This comprehensive handbook has explored the essential principles and strategies that empower entrepreneurs not just to survive but to thrive in a landscape marked by constant change and unpredictability.

From establishing the foundation of your entrepreneurial journey in the early chapters to mastering the art of excelling in uncertain times, this book has offered insights, tools, and wisdom to guide you on your path.

As we conclude this comprehensive handbook for entrepreneurs, remember that your journey is an ongoing adventure. Entrepreneurship is not a destination but a lifelong pursuit. The lessons and strategies shared here will serve as your guiding light. Embrace the unknown, view challenges as stepping stones to success, and maintain resilience in the face of adversity.

Your vision, innovation, and unwavering commitment have the potential not only to drive your personal success but also to make a profound impact on society and the wider world. The entrepreneurial spirit is a dynamic force for positive change, and the future is shaped by those who dare to venture into uncharted territories.

Continue to learn, adapt, and innovate. Foster a culture of continuous improvement, and never shy away from embracing failure as a valuable learning experience. The world eagerly awaits your entrepreneurial energy, creativity, and dedication to create meaningful change.

As you embark on your entrepreneurial odyssey, may this comprehensive handbook be your trusted companion, offering guidance and inspiration whenever you need it. Cultivate success in uncertainty, and let your entrepreneurial spirit lead the way. Your journey is destined to be an extraordinary and transformative one.

www.ingramcontent.com/pod-product-compliance
Lightning Source LLC
Chambersburg PA
CBHW062356290526
45794CB00005B/2251